Pam

Endogo book 4

Published by Crossbridge Books
Worcester
© Crossbridge Books 2025

ISBN 978-1-916945-13-5

British Library Cataloguing Publication Data. A catalogue record for this book is available from the British Library.

CROSSBRIDGE
BOOKS

Pam

Endogo book 4

by R M Price-Mohr

Vocabulary for book 4:

about
as
break
catch
climbing
fall
help
her
jumps
lemur
little
over
Pam
She/She
starts
suddenly/Suddenly
that
tree
twig
wants

Foreword for teachers

These books have been developed for older beginner readers. The research-based approach focuses on the recognition of just 100 key words that together make up approximately two-thirds of all reading matter in English.

For each new book, twenty new words are introduced and listed at the beginning of each book The new vocabulary for each book should be introduced to the learner in such a way that they will be able to recognise them at sight <u>before</u> reading the book. It is recommended that this is achieved through playing with the printed words. In the first instance, this should be by having two sets of printed and separated words in large font (minimum 20 point) that the beginner reader can match. It is crucial that the teacher continuously verbalise the words, and they may point to significant features in words, firstly the initial letters and secondly to any other distinctive features, to assist with the matching. Following this, the word recognition can be reinforced in games such as bingo, dominoes, snap, Pelmanism etc.

It is crucial that the teacher continue to verbalise the words during all the games, and the teacher should draw attention to the first letter of words and sound out that initial letter for the beginner.

Some temptations to avoid:

- Do not ask the reader to sound out all the individual letters of a word – only the initial letter has value at this stage for reading.
- Do not test the reader to see if they can recognise any of the words by telling you what they say – this should become obvious during the games; remember that visual recognition is not the same thing as verbalising what is seen.

This is Pam the endogo.

She is climbing a fruit tree.

She looks about her as she climbs.

She can see a little lemur.

Max wants to climb up too.

Suddenly, a small twig starts to break.

Pam can see that she will fall.

Max can see that she will fall too.

The little lemur wants to help.

Suddenly, the lemur jumps over to catch Pam.

Pam, Max, and the lemur are happy.

High Frequency Words:

about
as
help
her
jump
little
over
she
that
tree
want

Word Patterns:

_ing   looking
       eating
       going
       climbing
_all   fall
       all
       small
_ee   see
       tree

www.ingramcontent.com/pod-product-compliance
Lightning Source LLC
LaVergne TN
LVHW010316070426

835510LV00024B/3405